A
Husband's
Notes
about
Her

A
Husband's
Notes
about
Her

Fictions
by
Eve Merriam

Macmillan Publishing Co., Inc.
New York

Macmillan Publishing Co., Inc.
866 Third Avenue, New York, N.Y. 10022
Collier Macmillan Canada, Ltd.

Library of Congress Cataloging in Publication Data

Merriam, Eve.
A husband's notes about her.

I.   Title.
PS3525.E639H8   811'.5'4   75-25973
ISBN 0-02-584350-8

First Printing 1976

Printed in the United States of America

With grateful acknowledgment to
the MacDowell Colony for the gift of time.

These "notes" (poetic, fictional, documentary) are akin to anthropological field notes, as the male persona attempts to examine patterns of female culture.

In seeking to understand her behavior, he observes her in her native habitat, seeking clues in her territorial imperatives, in her language, dress, the way she looks and smells, her dreams, fantasies, furniture, eating habits, reading habits, the way she sits, shops, places bets, makes love, talks on the telephone.

During the course of his investigation, his own fears and fantasies are uncovered. As the notes leave off, one hopes that perhaps the great divide of the sexual gap has been lessened by their revealing themselves to one another.

E. M.

Contents

A
Husband's
Notes
about
Her

S + He

she is an S
sinuous   ladyslippering

He
I am He
my voice goes out
He heil   he heel   he stamp myself indelible
my He deeds   my He doings
what a wondrous work is I–He Man

sss
sssss
little bubbles of s escape
rippling the mirror
imperfections
                sssssss
what is she whispering
what is she hiding from he/me

        what

            isssss

                    s
                ssssshe
                    s

She Calls Me on the Telephone

ring! ring! bbring she orders
thinging me

an extra loaf
a double quart
oh and would you mind picking up
a can a case a crate a crane hoist
too heavy for her to carry so will I

Equal! she screams equalbeakqual talons the same
she wants to eagle fly as high
as man but can't because she's so bowed down by all the
chickenshit   she squeaksquawks
she yardputters   she squats
wingpulls   featherplucks

Well   equal yourself I tell her fetchyourself
the ladder the jack the load

Oh no she simps you'll have to
my muscles aren't made for heaving lifting not at haul

Okay so I'm bigger and stronger   right?

Wrong   she airies   infuriates with her illogicalilies
Physical strength is unimportant she wafts rne
Screw musclepower
today everything's done by machines
Physical strength is
irrelephant

Okay baby get yourself a breadwinning machine
a fucking goddamn machine

She Talks on the Telephone
to Her Girl Friends

He did
oh no
he really did
I can't believe it
of course they're all the same
who do we know for her
there must be somebody
she's too good for him but anyway

   The martears
       the goodesses
           the dainty diviners
deigning to descend

When I Come Home Late

It was traffic
or the boss kept me
but she looks at me
like she's finding lipstick on my collar

Only sometimes
it's worse when
she shrugs and says
"So you're late so what
I kept everything hot
what more could you want?"

Nothing   I shake my head   nothing at all

"You never talk to me," she yaps
"you never really want to talk
not any more
you never did—"

Not now   please   I'm tired   I'm hungry
I want to forget this whole lousy day

"It's never time," she bangs the plate on the table

All right I say let's talk and I put my fork down
What do you want to talk about

"Forget it," she flounces into the kitchen
"it doesn't matter."

Come on   I say   let's get it over with   now you
   started it

"I started it," she snorts
"that's a laugh   I started it he tells me"
she confides to the ceiling over my head

and we go to bed
and I nudge her in the crack
with my big toe
and say   come on honey don't you want to talk a little
and she says "Not now please," she pleads
"I'm tired   I had a head day ache"
do you want me to get you an aspirin I ask
"Please please leave me alone," she pleads
"stop pestering me"
and she flops over onto her side
and I'm there
like a flounder
with one eye
staring up at the ceiling

only sometimes it's even worse
when she sighs and says
"Okay   let's go"
            let's get it over with
            let's drive the kids to the beach and hurry up and
                  swim
            and get out of the wet ugh suits and dry and back
                  home
she's clopped out for me like a sack of cement
for me to slit
hard to make an opening
a few grains trickle out
then more
finally
I pour
what the hell
it's in there

Her Shopping List

olives stuffed with
virgin dreams

1 father-lover
1 husband-child

Objects to Be Included in the
Female Time Capsule

A maple rocking chair she purchased at auction because it was a replica of her grandmother's that she loved when she was a little girl and always wanted to have one of her own. She can't wait to fetch it home, goes to the expense of hauling it in a taxi, rearranges all the furniture in the living room around it, and then never sits in it at all.

A large hatbox containing a feather boa, taking up half the top shelf of the hall closet.

Throw it away or give it to the Good Will, I urge.

No, it might come back into style, she insists.

But you're allergic to feathers, I remind her.

I know, she says, what does that have to do with it?

A voluminous canvas shopping bag that she has made herself, because, she claims, all the ready-bought ones are never sturdy or large enough. The feature of her design is an inside zippered compartment where she keeps, not her wallet or keys, but a folded up smaller canvas bag, in case, she explains, she doesn't need all the space in the big one.

How She Reads the Newspaper

a headline first
the weather box
amusements
sale at a store
recipe
obits
society
another headline
another sale
tv and radio listings
cartoon on the editorial page
book review
carryover from a page one story she then
goes back to page one and skims the beginning

Her Daily Chores

Wash

    clothes   dishes   stains of memory

Iron

    shirts   pillowcases   sighs

Straighten out

    drawers   shelves   him

She Clips from the Newspaper:

SAN FRANCISCO, Oct. 20 (UPI)—
A student who teased a friend
for losing a game of dominoes
to a girl was stabbed to death
by the friend in his high school
classroom   yesterday.   Stanley
Blaine, 17 years old, died of
knife wounds in the heart and
left arm. Charles L. Harris, 16,
was arrested at his home shortly
after the stabbing at Woodrow
Wilson High School.

Her scrawl alongside: "This should go on the sports page, shouldn't it? To be beaten by a female—a fate no worse than death."

I almost miss her added comment in the margin: "Would it kill you to quit watching football on teevee and stenching up the room with cigar smoke?"

What She Eats When She Is Alone

tuna fish
a scrambled egg
whole wheat wafers
a sliver of devil's food cake
a grabbing gobbling look at the rest of the cake

She Beholds Herself in the Mirror

I love you   you're a movie star
oh God I'm growing old
my eyes are good   so is my skin
and my cheekbones
what's that mole   cancer?
I don't want to be my mother
save me from it
ghastly beginning of a mustache
and scrawny turkey skin on my neck
I need a little softer light
if I tint my hair I'm afraid it will grow in coarser
already there's gray in my pubic
kinkier   thicker
my eyes are fine and my smile

Her mouth wobbles and she turns to me
in need
in desperate
and she comes almost too fast for me

Afterwards she dresses and puts on
a ring
a necklace
a belt
she circles herself
circe to her own sorceress
belonging to
her own private world
her smile that moana
a moat
no drawbridge
no way for me to enter
her mind

Frontal View

She has decided to go to a Thursday evening sketch class at the local women's center. An inexpensive pastime, and I don't mind eating alone. When she returns after the first session, I ask politely How did it go?

For answer, she hands over the spiral-bound pad I have purchased for her. The top page is full of scribbling; I can barely make it out: "For centuries women could not become medical students because they were forbidden to study anatomy. So too women artists were not permitted into life classes and could not paint from a model directly.

The Male Nude, Seated

Sits naked on the edge of the sofa, testicles forming a stubby pin cushion as he leans forward. But notice, class: his pinhead is not sharp, it droops like a tape measure that has been bound up in the sewing basket, held tight with an elastic band, and when the band is undone the measure can unreel, but the cloth inchmarks retain their memory of curl. To be straightened out, pressure must be applied. Lightly at first. Approach, class, and observe: the veins marbled like steak; the web, the skein of outer skin, droopy as a long skirt or an old-fashioned reticule, dangling, pouty; now feel the solid bits inside that skate around like ball bearings or unborn chicken eggs that will never hatch."

I am seething as I flip the pages of the pad over. Blank. And where is the drawing you did, I ask.

Oh, she says, the model didn't show up.

When She Is with Another Woman

No matter whether the woman is like her
or most unlike
they stop talking as I enter the room
schoolgirls caught in naughty confidences
sneaky exchanges
—I shouldn't tell you but I do—
their heads turned in
almost touching
like parts of a valentine
like buttock halves
not open and manly

Polarity

She asks me to return a book to the library for her. Naturally she hasn't told me that it is overdue; I pay the fine for her and glance at the page where she has left a marker.

"Emperor penguin: the most truly Antarctic of all birds. No nest. After the egg is laid, soon after the sea ice forms in autumn, the male takes charge of it, carrying it on the top of the feet, warmed by a fold of skin on his belly. While the male fasts, the female travels, perhaps many miles, across the sea ice in order to reach open water and feed. Towards the end of the sixty-day incubation period she returns to relieve the male and feed the chick. The males then disperse after their long fast."*

I remove the marker with her jottings:

> papa
> brooding
> over the
> blank whiteness
> of his days
>
> what is there to note
> when it's always
> the same flat horizon
>
> sit
> waiting for her
> to come back
> from the diverse world
> where things happen

* Sparks and Soper, *Penguins*. Angus and Robertson, 1968.

like to change places
if he could be the one to
bear the young

then he'd be out now
splashing around
and she'd be
stuck with it
solid

On the Shelf

An ardent feminist complains that *Peter Pan* should not be featured on the local library shelf, since Wendy plays too subordinate a character. Perhaps we can look forward to a series of ecumenical consensus tales:

> Once upon a time in Sherwood Forest there lived a wonderful man named Robin Hood.
>
> He took from the somewhat affluent to give to the slightly less affluent.
>
> Among his trusty companions were Middle John, a medium-sized fellow, and Friar Schwartz.
>
> Robin and his band of merry fellows cooked their supper around the campfire. Depending on whose turn it was, they ate
>
> > rice and beans,
> > enchiladas,
> > moo goo gai pan,
> > gazpacho,
> > hogmaws and fatback,
> > caviar and blini,
> > sourdough biscuits,
> > smoked eel,
> > boeuf Bourguignon,
> > pickled seaweed,
> > or fried banyan root.
>
> The Sheriff of Nottingham set out to capture Robin Hood, and challenged him to a bow-and-arrow contest.
>
> When Robin won first prize, he took off his disguise and revealed himself as Maid Marian, the first Black woman in space.

Tracking Her

What is still permissible to dislike in her sex now that it has become unpardonable to speak against them?

My nextdoor neighbor says Girl and I correct him; never never do I myself indulge in Gal, Babe, Jane, Doll, Chick. Worthy as these Mses may all be to function as chairpersons of the board, they nevertheless are not quite Einsteins or even Edisons.

They go to the racetrack and bet on Dark Victory in the eighth, not because they have made a study of Jack's Green Card or The Racing Form, but because once upon a time they dated a boy named Victor who had dark brown eyes.

Sometimes Dark Victory turns into a longshot winner. I am aghast and thrilled for her; she, however, is entirely nonchalant as she goes to cash in her two-dollar ticket. She's not in the least surprised: she knew it would come in.

When the horse loses, she is furious; it is a personal insult to her until she recovers to furnish a scientific explanation: Victor's eyes may have been blue.

The Missing Half

I never know from one day to the next
how she will greet me
be my mate
or a formal acquaintance

Is that because she is always Persephone
six months underground with Pluto father of the dark
dark steeping deep
six months above with Demeter mothering meadows of
milky mild wildweed

Is she angry because I can never be her mother
as she can many times be mine?

When She Sits

At first she crosses her ankles and clasps her hands
in her lap in the traditional ladylike pose.

Then, as to exorcise with a gesture all that past history
of protection, she spreads her thighs apart
or flings one leg athwart the other.

And with her right hand she cups her left elbow
in a kind of bodily self-greeting.

I wonder if she realizes it makes a rudimentary cradle shape?

Breastworks

1

giant grapes to pluck
ripe in every season
a Gauguin dream
of Tahiti to taste
over and over and

2

stroke
encircle the nipple
the smooth plain begins to pucker
tiny craters on the moon extrude
put forth their Lilliput lunar towers
as my fingers
real estate magnate
make them rise

3

proffer my single breast my prick
to pull on
while back to the born moment
I suckle
at the double font

After the First Time

We were lolling on the rumpled sheets, sweat cooling off, sharing a filtertip cigarette, the ashtray balancing on her belly. As was to be expected, we exchanged confidences, and as with all her sex, she was eager to start.

Telling me about all her previous lovers, I was jealous of only two, because I couldn't comprehend them: the one who doted on her hairy thighs (he didn't like her shaving to wear a bathing suit) and the one who lapped at her menstrual blood. If they had both been the same person, it is possible I might have been less disturbed.

My confidences to her were more guarded.

She didn't seem to notice any omissions, scarcely paid attention to the names, interrupting to ask Was she thinner than I am? Was her hair longer? Did she wrap her legs around you this way? And the ashtray would slide off, and we would begin again.

Just as well.

How could I tell her that the most erotic experience of my youth was the time I got a cinder in my eye, walking home from Junior High; the more I kept blinking, the more it dug in: gritty, painful, until my mother raised the lid, held the crescent flap of flesh between her index and middle finger, and then delicately, deliberately, her tongue licked across my eyeball and lifted the cinder free.

Her Smells after Sex

fishbroth
skim off the top   scupper
albumin   eggwhite
stiffening the sheet
running down her leg
viscous   thick enough for a soup stock

she sits on the toilet while
I lift my prick into the sink
and wash it gently
pat it
put it into my shorts
"Oh let me do it," she reaches out from the seat
"dear sweet creatures," she kisses my balls through the cloth
and she's ready for more   right now or if not
she has energy enough to swim a lake
or climb a mountain
or clean a closet

Her Fantasy

is to shoot automobiles. She envisions herself as the head of an international youth gang, they run around at midnight, hitting into parked cars, out on the street, highways, in garages, wherever they can get away with it. She is Miss Supershot, pow. Take that. Another chrome body bites the dust, fender agonizes and crumples.

She ignores the fact that no matter how many guerilla actions she engages in, the registration of cars has gone up thirty-nine per cent in the last ten years, according to a Wall Street Journal index. She'll kill em all, she vows.

And what if there are always more where the old assembly line came from?

Ah, into River Rouge with her Ecocommandos, young, hirsute, fondling, and she their queenly buddypal in the commune. Attack the Ford factories! Bombs for combustion engines! Grenades to promote grassy lawns and country lanes!

How will we transport ourselves, the voice of reason inquires.

Ah ah, transport ourselves on wings of joy, she orges. On our own gloriously muscled limbs, Blakean creatures. Or, if we must, by trolleys, trains, helicopters. Steam-driven. Or truly horse-powered, stallions galloping, mares' manes flying.

She could never manage a business.
If I die first, let her hire a good accountant.

What Do You Want for
Your Birthday?

I ask, and she shakes her head,
murmuring sweetly,
"I have everything I want."
Nuzzling me,
"I have you."

Pretending as I do to sleep,
she does not notice that I see her
when she floats up after midnight
and drifts to the island causeway.

She crosses over to the other side:

   the other side
   where there is
   a discharge
   from the penis
   for a few days
   every month;

   it discommodes
   certain men,
   most simply
   don a
   waterproof jock strap
   and go about
   their usual
   business.

The discharge is
odorless,
but there is a fantasy
among the women
that it has a peculiar
odor and some of them
prefer not to
suck their men
during that period.

Consequently,
these men become cranky,
swollen with
ill humor,
and so the story goes round

that the men during their time
are moody,
changeable,
unreliable;
one should not

conduct important
or money matters
when they are
in their discharge.

Graffiti in the Ladies' Room

When there is no one around to notice, I take a look inside the ladies' room.

Sanitary napkins/tampon dispenser.
Lipstick.
Cologne.
Feminine hygiene spray.

Graffiti in the stalls:

Alma Elder is a loving lay.

Fighting for Peace
    is
Fucking for Charity

Mammy set me on your knee,
I'm pregnant and he
Won't marry me.

Buy INCEST—a game the whole
family can play.

I think my boyfriend has
homosexual tendencies.
What should I do to help him?
Answer please.

Castrate him!

Don't let him fuck you up the asshole.

All boys are—some just don't try to
hide it.

Be excellent in bed—try the modern
dance to help you become Nubile.

Ask him to introduce you to some of
his boyfriends!

Get rid of your virginity so you won't
be afraid of *real* men.

Accept him as he is and find another
boyfriend.

Send him to a doctor you dope
(after speaking to him about it of
course)

RAPE ME PLEASE

Jay Kimball
is the worst fuck
in Kansas

The language is harsher than I expected.
Somehow I expect only men to think in terms of
lay and get laid, like pay and being paid; no nonsense,
in and out, wham bang, thank you ma'am.

"To sleep with" is more feminine, graceful,
implying to wake up with, to be comforted,
lingering, loving.

Scent

Her favorite perfume is a combination of roses and lilies, sickeningly sweet as a funeral parlor. The heavy scent is unbearable; it almost makes me retch.

Why do you use it? I ask.

"To make myself more attractive to you," she says and dabs behind her earlobes, under her arms, the tips of her nipples, between her thighs, the inside of her elbows and inner wrists, her navel, the cleft in her buttocks, the arches of her feet.

The Presence of Her Absence

She puts placemats on the table
and after breakfast
crumbs them
sponges them
shakes them in the air to dry
and stores them away
in a drawer of the dining room chest
behind the silverware box

> *her diaphragm*
> *washed patted powdered*
> *rolled flat into its plastic case*
> *tucked out of sight*
> *back of the bandaids and eyedrops*

When she isn't home
I place the mats on the table
and they stay

All that in and out of cupboards
catching releasing
why play hide and seek
let things be where you can see them
where you can get to them
whenever you want them
any time
right up front

Half and Half

What kind of Doppelgänger can she be for me—
my double in what ways

She does not shave her face
she does not dress left

two upper balls
shoved into jock strap of a bra
how does it feel to be fondled
to bounce
to burst free

nipples erect
little hairs around
I close my eyes and stroke
thinking of her as an airline stewardess
my hostess serving me snacks   drinks
tingling
her hair swinging in my face as she bends over for my order
slapping teasing me
she peels off her uniform
holds up her breasts to me to nibble to sip
it's de luxe not peanuts
but macadamias   Hawaiian grand tour

M into W

M	W
standing	sitting
pointer	dome
tower	cave

W as an inverted M.
Vice versa.

In the nighttime sky, Cassiopeia's Chair: summer months the shape is a W as it hangs below Ursa Major, the great bear. An M in winter as it rides above.

Who moves the chair?
Who forms a lap?

Ideas of Perspective

M	W
a wheel	a globe
a car	a fruit
a highway	a branch
a city	a tree
a nation	an orchard
a hemisphere	a continent
a globe	a body

Four-Letter Words

Mind	Weft
Make	Wait
Move	Wear
Mold	Weir

The Things That Are Her
Ladies' Gentletalia

purse   snatch
pocket   pick hole   daisy eye   ray
panties   lace fringe see through
eye snatch u
closing in for the
what

her lips pursed
I can't catch twat she is saying

Comb
comb
comb her wild combers her shuddering waves   her
spring leaking onto me
velva velour plushfung
cask with a bunghole
rush to come

Whatever I give her she
takes
and   many times
it is almost
enough

What's missing?

Ah, she lifts off to her side,
it must be the secret of life
if we knew what was missing
we wouldn't have to spend our lives
looking   lacking   fooking   for nooking

Porn

I tell her about the two sailors in Times Square.
Hey, says one, let's go into this store—they've got a sale on some good pornography.
Aw, says the second, I haven't even got a pornograph to play it on.
"That's a sweet story," she shakes her head, "and sort of sad."
She's ready to take the second sailor home and feed him up.

Presumably women are not turned on by porn.
They require romance, soft music, tender touch, voice speaking their name over and feeling over.
Yet sometimes I have caught her staring at the Playboy centerfold. To compare herself only?

When we have gone to explicit films I can hardly wait till we get back home to strip.
She is obdurate, then lunges for me.
I have to watch or she will bite: it is not gentle play on her part, she is really searching for vulnerable places, eager to break the skin.
Hey, cut it out, I try laughing at her.
"You were so hot you couldn't wait, so what's wrong?"
Nothing, you'll see, and I pump away.
But it's not good.
It's like trying to make it with a vampire, you don't really want to get into that scene.
She's panting when we finish, pleased with herself.
"Oh," she gloats, "I hate it when we go to one of those movies and the bodies on the screen give you the hots.
You need that jazzing up you crock don't you"

Maybe I do sometimes. But I think she does too. Those surveys on female attitudes are leftover Victorian crud. It's easier if we suppose women don't get aroused by porn.

Tidier, if we have only our own sex to control.

I watch her closely when we go to the next Danish film and then to a nude stage play. I could swear she's focusing her eyes more on the women than the men. I see her breasts heaving, the nipples hardening, her face flushes.

Is there some kind of lesbian trip going on that I don't know about?

I'm watching the guys on stage, sure, curious to see if their peckers can keep it up.

They don't turn me on though. I'm not getting any jollies out of the guys.

Her Private Collection

In the bottom drawer of her bureau, I find five well-thumbed picture postcards, hidden under a pile of bikini panties.

They are museum cards. Miniature reproductions.
One is Seurat's Woman with a Parasol, thimble-waisted, pannier-skirted.
Assembled with thousands of pastel dots: fragmented, signifying nothing until you stand away from it far enough.

Next, a photograph of an Eastern woman in purdah, swathed top to toe in black, entirely blotted out, not even eye-slits in the thick veiling.
She has been captured by the photographer as she walks on a trafficked street and balances, on top of her head, a sewing machine.

The third card is Scheile's brutalized brunette, wearing only a mustard-yellow lace mantilla and knee-high stockings to match. She is standing up, her legs outspread, hairy. Hairy.

Next in line is Matisse's woman of the nineteen-twenties, with bobbed hair, in negligee, elbow on table, hand propped to cheek, lips and fingernails tinted like the weakly red goldfish swimming inside the bowl she is gazing at; the fish are tiny as tears, and the woman's eyes are blankly round as the fishbowl.

Finally, there is Fuseli's Nightmare: the woman in white draped over the mattress, swarthy demon squatting on her torso while a horse's head with glaring eyeballs looms from the left.

On the reverse side of the last card in the pile, "Now that you have unearthed all my self-portraits, which one of the five do you think resembles me the most?"

Dream of Two Sexes

Chicago UPI Wire Service Story:

"A sleep study reports that women tend to dream about clothing, houses, furniture and schools while men tend to dream about money, automobiles, foreign countries and trees."

> I have driven my car to Spain
> where I find
> moneyfruit growing on trees
> it drips into my mouth
> but the skin puckers
>
> while she
> rubs the furniture
> with her pantyhose running
> and sniffs at the school blackboard
> chalk in her hand
> trembling to write a dirty word
> it comes out EL O
> *Him*
> _Himmel_

She Follows the Embroidery Directions

The piece of cloth
to be pricked
is first stretched

and then bound
with an inner
and an outer

rigid hoop,
thereby creating
an area

of concentration;
practice
will demonstrate

just how
the material
should be pulled,

for if over-
taut: then
the hoops

spring out
and it all
collapses.

When a Homosexual Imitates Her

he uses italic superlatives
the *darlingest* dress
the *cutest* little restaurant
simply the *most dreadful dreariest* film of *all time*

but she doesn't really talk that way except
when she's mimicking a fag

Why does she hate them so?
On the party surface they get along fine
quoting old musical comedy lyrics
and carrying on about Joan and Judy and dahling and
Pe-tah
and she's pleased that he notices her dress
and matching pantyhose and lipstick
and he in turn is pleased
that she covets his bodyshirt
they could be twins   so cozy do they carry on
but the minute we leave and are on our way home
she lets out the breath she's been holding all evening long
Disgusting
her snaky ssss hisses out
she could flay him with her darting poisoning tongue

What is it
what's the threat
if I'm not upset by him
if my manhood isn't shaken
then why should she be raging like a Maenad

what is the ancient
magnetic pole?

Gay Time

There's one, she'll announce as we're crossing the street.

How can she tell so quickly?
He isn't wearing the single earring sign, or a pendant, ornate belt buckle, oversized rings. There isn't the pursed mouth, hand on hip, arched buttocks.
I've seen pants that fit a lot tighter.
Nor is the walk mincing as if avoiding a tiny pile of dogshit set directly in front of where each foot is about to step.

She will point out a man dressed in a jacket with a print lining, perhaps, or an ascot scarf. The colors are never primary, but tend to combinations of chartreuse and navy blue; magenta and orange; rust with purple.
Perfect for powder room wallpaper, she will say bitchily, even though she herself has bought a skirt in a similar combination and has proudly displayed the label: that of a well known designer who is equally well known as a homosexual.

Why does she do it?
And why is her hairdresser one too?
Why does she apologize that after all they're the best in the business . . .
Given their bent, I can understand that they enjoy playing around cutting out polka dots or fluffing up curls, but why does she let them take her for a footstool in their dream-queen parlor?

I wouldn't stand for any butch babe waiting on me in the clothing store, hitching up my trouser leg or taking my measure in any way whatever. And I wouldn't let some dyky dame act as my barber; what could she know about the stiffness of my beard, how careful you have to be right under the chin, it's easy to nick and draw blood. For all I know, with her grudge against her birthright, she might want to let the razor slip a little bit on purpose.

But there's my wife, encouraging the gay blades.

They're putting a double whammy on her: persuading that they're helping her look her most "feminine," and at the same time they're copying her, aping her in the most vulgar way.

The transvestite lifts only the trashiest bits from the repertoire. Swinging a pocketbook by the handles.

Flipping a wrist.

Tripping about on ankle-strap high heels.

Flashing a boob.

Which comes first: the lady in the mirror or the fag-mime?

In times of stress, watch her resort to imitating a fag imitating a female. *Don't criticize me or I'll cry.*

Under siege, she exaggerates herself into an ersatz female: patting her hair, fingering her ring, clasping her purse, adjusting her straps, pulling at her neckline, smiling vacantly all the while. *Why should I have to learn all those dry facts about what makes the motor run? Some nice man will take care of it for me won't he.* And her voice goes up half a register, squeaky as Marilyn Monroe or Jackie Onassis portrayed by a five o'clock shadow.

Her laugh gets shriller and her glance bobs around the room, looking for a getaway, darting, climbing, like a hamster let loose and clawing up the curtains.

Put it back with the shredded bits of lettuce and the play-wheel in its cage.

But plant a homosexual in her path and she eyes him level. Stares directly at him, unafraid.

As a white Alabama landowner has more in common with a black Alabama sharecropper than the most liberal poor pale Northerner can ever hope to profess, so these two comprehend one another. They can exchange looks of immediate empathy, enmity. Twinned in part of their personalities.

Neither one of them is accepted into the all-male club.
Trying to find ways to sneak around the rules, they know each other's tricks and can despise and be despised.
Some nice man will take me in so long as I snuggle up to him.
Me too.
So long as I roll over wag my tail sit up and play tricks.
Me see me do.

Recognizing one another from Pseudopersonland: grownups not admitted.
Where she can be a little girl clomping around the bedroom in Mommy's high heels, how cute that the shoes are so big on her. Or try on Daddy's floppy shirt and let the sleeves dangle all the way down like great elephant trunks come to scoop her up.
Where he can imitate Judy Garland in her tuxedo jacket, black tights, high silk hat and cane, wouldn't you swear he's got her to the life?

The life of surface gestures, of warm shallows and backwater bays.

> Mon semblable,
> ma soeur.

Tucked in Her Bottom Drawer:
The Loose-Leaf Lectures

The collection of picture postcards is gone, and in their stead, pages from a loose-leaf book. Do they present quotations from some lecture series she has been attending, or are they her own remarks?

"As H———, the cultural anthropologist, discovered, women had not been allowed to learn how to read and write. If they had been, they would then have participated in government, law, professions, religion, business, science, art, civil institutions.
Therefore they developed an oral literature only.
H——— has been able to tape and translate some examples.

"This one is from the ancient kingdom of the UKPENS, where the women were restricted to a pen or fold, a sort of cross between pig——— and play———.

> SPOONFED: *Chant for a Dance Around the Fire*
> There is a spoon
> and here is my mouth.
> Wide,
> wider my hunger.
>
> I bend to the spoon
> round-edged,
> shallow,
> a place to lick.
> What is the spoon?
> Is it you?

"H——— has also a song from the MAGAPIES, a matrilocal grouping.

> Bake me as bread.
> I rise, I spread.
> Consume me too quickly
> and you are dead.
> But if you delay
> a single day
> I become moldy
> and poison you
> or so stiff
> you cannot
> cut me with
> your knives.

(H——— was unable to get the last part of the translation to rhyme as it does in the original. H——— apologized.)

"H——— went on to discuss the LABBIAS. In the Labbia tribe, where there had been an ancient revolt of the females that was put down brutally, the women revenged themselves by mating with animals and taunting the men with their love calls. Examples follow.

Me me me ow ow
come now noooooowwwww
cat with your furry tail
you palpate
your pink tongue licking over hairs one by one
let your clawing teeth pierce me
me me ow ow now nooowww come noooww

Oof oof roo roo
dog dog roll over me
slaver your jaws
spittle
I savor

Oheee oheee ohiii ohiii
great bird
fly me to your nest
hold me in your heat
hatch me
as no man ever can

Roar rrrrroarrrr mmmmmorrrre
sea-lion
out of the deep
rise for me
thrust me on your back
leap into the waves
shudder
rise up and up

then rump over rocks
slide upon the shore
roar roarr mmmorrrre
mmmmmmm
mmmmmm
ah
beach me on your side

Oralania

"Lacking historical records, the women of Oralania cut patterns for their behavior out of fabric.

From their old clothes, they make syllable patches to be sewn together into a comforter against the cold and darkness.

HUS	BAND
MAT	TRESS
CHIL	DREN

NUR	SING
COO	KING

POT	A	TO

And after the cover is worn out, they rip the patches apart and resew the shreds into rag rugs, soft padding against the hard core of Earthfloor.

HUS   HIS

MAT

TRESS

D   I   S

CHIL   BAN

D   R   E   N

NUR   COO   SING KING

A POT TO

"Since they have no tradition, they invent what they can. Lipstick containers out of old male cartridge cases. Fairy tales redrawn. Example: The Fisherman's Wife. They tell it and pass it on down as

The Fisherwoman's Husband

Once there was a poor fisherwoman and her husband. They lived in a hut on a rocky cliff. Early each morning the fisherwoman arose and went out in the boat while the househusband mended nets and stirred the iron pot. One day the fisherwoman caught a magic fish. 'If you do not eat me, but throw me back into the sea, I will grant you three wishes.'
The fisherwoman's husband begged, 'Oh, do please ask for a larger house. This one is so cramped, I must work on my hands and knees and the roof leaks.'
Instantly they were in a pleasant cottage with a garden.
The fisherwoman was contented, but her husband soon began to grumble. 'The sun pours in and fades the carpet and there are weeds in the garden, I must get down on my hands and knees to pull them out. I wish we could live in a mansion with caretakers.'
Immediately they were in a splendid mansion overlooking a fertile valley below. 'I like being king of the hill,' said the husband, 'but I would like to be on top of everything—I wish to be Pope, president, professor with tenure, Pentagon chief, head of the banking cartel, owner of offshore oil deposits, producer of multi-millia spectaculars on stage, screen, land, sea, air and under—'
'Fool!' the magic fish interrupted. 'You have finally

gone too far. Don't you know that only a woman can achieve what you have asked for?' And they were put back in their hut where the fisherwoman fried her husband for supper.

"The tribe of VENERA, where the older women inhabit young male lovers.

The staple of their diet is the mango, which is grown in hundreds of varieties with subtle differences of aroma and taste. Wrinkles and spots on the skin are not marks of decay but an indication of ripeness. Sweetest when slightly over-ripe, the pulpy flesh is orange-colored as the hunter's or harvest moon in autumn; it surrounds a very large fibrous pit, and can be spooned out or eaten with the fingers.

Translation of one of the songs of Venera, whether composed by a young male or an older woman is not known.

> A gray hair has fallen across my robe.
> Crawling spider,
> I hasten to brush it off.
>
> Time goes by.
>
> Many gray hairs fall across my robe.
> I brush them tenderly.
> Are not the webs of spiders beautiful?

"H——— also has from the SIBYLLAS a brief collection of riddles, adages, omens, forecasts, invective.

A sample riddle: What is a man to me?
Answer: three things, air   nothing   and death.
    Air   I need him to breathe
    Nothing   for having him I do not need him as air
        cannot be seen
    Death   for having it I do not need him and I do not
        breathe and nothing of death can be known

Adage: If a man be caught in the river, the river is unclean
    and he is not to be eaten

Another—Separate toilets = separate shames

Omen: The stars are scattered like our fathers who pricked
    our blood.
    When will the mother of earth come to relieve us?
        Relive us?
    Mother of earth has been made deaf and cannot hear
        our cry.
    Mother of earth has been blinded and cannot see our
        growth.
    Mother of earth has had her tongue ripped out and
        cannot speak for herself.
    Her pen is her tongue, her ink is her menstrual blood.

"Next time H——— is going to show us slides of women's art: dishes, containers, pickle jars, wraps, all things enclosed that can be shattered and flung apart.

The Last of the Loose-Leaf Lectures

"The pygmy men of Central Africa grow to a height of about four feet. Most of them belong to African planters who have inherited pygmies from their fathers and will leave them to their sons along with the rest of their property.

Pygmies clear the bush, help with planting and harvesting, have no possessions of their own, save for a hide-sex of leaves or string and a piece of cloth that they may wear. They do not go to school. 'Pygmies are afraid of sunlight,' explains the owner of several coffee and corn plantations. They live in small round huts made of branches and leaves and sleep on pieces of bark, live principally on manioc roots and bananas and are severely undernourished.

'However,' states a New York Times dispatch from Baganou, a market town in the equatorial forest, 'change is beginning to penetrate. A few pygmies have settled down in hamlets along forest roads. These "civilized pygmies" build permanent houses with mud and sticks. They are beginning to wear clothes. Nevertheless, even the "civilized pygmies" are considered lesser beings.' 'We could not think of allowing pygmies—even with clothes—into church because they smell so bad,' a gardener for a lumber company said.

Occasionally the Ministry of Tourism has brought small groups of pygmies out of the forest to dance and give their lovely birdlike yodel for visitors. 'We can't do much with the little people because basically they're not interested in money and would rather stay in the woods,' a French travel agent said."

The pages and newsclip have been ripped, then put back together with scotch tape. A magic marker scrawl across the page:

The Pygmies Are Your Wife

The Blank Boxes

After that, the loose-leaf book contains no further reference to H———. There are only a series of doodles, diminishing in size, all the shapes rectangular and boxed-in. Around the edges, more of her scribbling: "Turkish folktales begin this way: 'Once there was and was not.' Folktales/Females. Fill in the blank boxes with husband's name, husband's occupation, husband's charge accounts, husband's bank references."

Her Menses

the month-mark
lunar
moth
flutter in the darkness
frail-beating   pale
beating
churning to yellow
as cream   as yolk
pinked
then red
red
smash

slashmark
her gash swollen   ,   inflamed
redeyed slit weeping in
the burning bush
fire fire
woe unto
all who come near
the smoke curls
singes the air
stand back   stand back   warn the firemen

No! No! Climb to me!
urges her smoking hair
her flesh sizzling

by moonlight   by monthly moonlight
she is Griselda in the tower
calling out to
take the ladder of my legs and rise to meet her

rescue her from the keep of her pent pulse
she leans over the casement window
her breasts engorged by the flood
of her red river surging

pleading to
carry her away on a magic carpet
oriental rug of
glistening dark red silken strands
tough-knotted
fringed in the burning bush

why do I resist?

The first time we made red love
the bed was smeared and
my thighs my belly my cheeks
the lobes of my ears
marked
as the Ancient of Days marked the
lintels of chosen doorways
I will take your firstborn
I will take your future strength
I will take you

the Ancient of Days become
a sibyl
skirted
sheathed on
a glistening dark red robe like
a caul
an envelope
an afterbirth
blood brew

commands me to sip of her sour red wine
she will drink me   drain me

I am brought into her world unwitting
drugged   dragged into the devil's dancing ring
the she-devil
deeper than the devil himself
roaring stamping gleaming
her red boots
her camp ground dripping with blood
red rain
fertilizing a crop I never sowed
I never sired
No sir
some buffalo stallion rhino bull some Ur-creature
not I

run to escape
through the burning woods
the blazing marsh
the dark red wilderness smoldering
the trees gashed with red ax marks

hack my way
out of the wild wet mess
red branches crashing
red leaves slippery in the red mud
red droppings of
deer shot in the darkness their flanks still hot and
quivering
feathers of birds wet dark streaking the sky
with their redstartle cries
red vine   red root strangling

out from the burning bush
break
out
out
into
thank God!
for the
rational
cool
electric
light
switch
of
the
manmade
world.

She is fearful only when the bleeding does *not* occur:
she is an anti-creature to me.

In Her Desk

Coupons for free samples and ten-cents-off sales that she has not cashed in, together with a flower-bordered pink leatherbound volume stamped in gold: "My Diary." The word *My* has been changed to *Public*.

Entry One:

>Our Advertising Director suggests that the new products division should be aware of the following copyrighted brand names before proposing anything for further laboratory samplings:
>
>KINDNESS is an activated conditioner for hair
>DAYLIGHT is a shampoo
>CONSORT is hair spray for men
>HAPPINESS is foam-in conditioning hair color
>EXCELLENCE is permanent shampoo-in color
>LOVING CARE is hair color lotion that washes away
>only the gray
>LOVE is an entire line of cosmetics
>NOTHING BUT THE TRUTH is a girdle
>THANK GOODNESS is a laundry soap
>FUTURE is an acrylic floor finish

Entry Two:

>Please be advised that our Advertising Director also doubles as high school guidance counselor: "Females," he advises, "are people whose lives we already know. It is unrealistic to permit young women to develop careers because ninety-three per cent will marry and take on those responsibilities."

Entry Three:

Psychology test, marketing research:

Show the class a picture of a woman pushing a baby carriage. Point out that there is no baby inside, but an outline of something else. What is it? Have them select the correct multiple choice answer from the following a, b, c list:

A. *A pile of dishes*

B. *A stack of cans*

C. *A skein of knitting*

Answer in back of book:

D. None of the above.

Her husband.

Entry without a Number

To Gaea, Hera, Juno, Athena, Minerva et sistera:

Dear Great Goddess ——— (fill in name),

We are conducting a study of outstanding Great Goddesses and sincerely hope you will assist us. Research on eminence among the greats has dealt almost exclusively with Great Gods; consequently, little information is available on goddesses who have achieved renown. More knowledge about the personality factors that make Goddesses Great will help in the recognition and development of the potential of future Great Goddesses.

For our study we are enlisting the cooperation of all those who have been honored by inclusion in *"She's She."* We are asking you to respond anonymously to the enclosed.

This same questionnaire has been used for a series of studies of Great Gods.

Thank you for your interest, and in return for your time and trouble, we are happy to send you the enclosed free giant can of foaming Ajax.

Olympia-Parnassus Institute for Personality
and Ability Testing

What to do: You will want to answer exactly and truly these questions that are planned to see what attitudes and interests you have as an outstanding Great Goddess. There are no "right" or "wrong" answers because everyone has the right to his own views.

DO NOT TURN PAGE UNTIL TOLD TO DO SO

I have the instructions for this test clearly in mind. (a) yes, (b) uncertain, (c) no.

I feel a bit nervous of wild animals even when they are in strong cages. (a) yes, (b) uncertain, (c) no.

I'd rather that the person I marry be socially admired than gifted in art or literature. (a) true, (b) uncertain, (c) false.

I like a friend (of my sex) who: (a) seriously thinks out his attitudes to life, (b) in between, (c) is efficient and practical in his interests.

I prefer reading: (a) a realistic account of military or political battles, (b) uncertain, (c) a sensitive, imaginative novel.

I believe firmly "the boss may not always be right, but he always has the right to be boss." (a) yes, (b) uncertain, (c) no.

I would rather stop in the street to watch an artist painting than listen to some people having a quarrel. (a) true, (b) uncertain, (c) false.

I am known as an "idea man" who almost always puts forward some ideas on a problem. (a) yes, (b) in between, (c) no.

My reserve always stands in the way when I want to speak to an attractive stranger of the opposite sex. (a) yes, (b) in between, (c) no.

If someone got mad at me, I would: (a) try to calm him down, (b) uncertain, (c) get irritated.

The use of foul language, even when it is not in a mixed group of male and female, still disgusts me. (a) yes, (b) in between, (c) no.

"Soon" is to "never" as "near" is to: (a) "nowhere," (b) "far," (c) "next."

As a young goddess-in-greatness trainee, were you ever encouraged to:

      (a) play with lightning bolts?
      (b) dress in wild asses' skins?
      (c) drink from a horn of plenty?

From Come to In

New York Times report, May 29, 1974:
Two psychologists at the University of Nevada have trained Washoe, a female chimpanzee, to use sign language. Her earliest words, in the order Washoe learned them:

Come-gimme
More
Up
Sweet
Go
Hear-listen
Tickle
Toothbrush
Hurry
Out
Funny
Drink
Sorry
Please
Food-eat
Flower
Cover-blanket
You
In

A Letter from Me

Dear Washoe,

Now that you and your human trainers are learning to communicate, perhaps you can help me with my wife.

Before you protest that this is too prodigious a task to take on, let me remind you that she is, after all, of the same sex as yourself.

You are bound to have much in common.

Perhaps you are more of a scratcher than she is, yet you both suckle. And she too likes bananas.

Watching her weight as she does, she tells me (boringly, repetitively) when I reach for a beer and a hunk of sharp cheese to munch on with the teevee news, that a banana is the perfect evening snack, that it is extremely easy to digest so no worry about nightmares, and that it is very filling yet contains only a hundred calories.

How can I respond? When I tell her that a banana may satisfy *her* hunger pangs, which face it are slighter than mine, just look at her height and weight, a banana won't do for me and besides it's mushy, nothing to sink my teeth into, then she says in her loftiest tone, "*cheese,* cheese is one of the highest cholesterol foods, and while Dr. Jean Mayer's nutrition column finds no *absolute* corollary between high cholesterol and heart attacks, still. . . ." her voice trails off into a shrug, one of her habits that I find particularly irritating.

Wouldn't you think, dear Washoe, that as a grown man, I should be entitled to pick any kind of snack I want without consulting her? And if it's high cholesterol, so what? It's my heart attack, not hers.

Tell me, why does she manage to make me feel guilty: as if, what kind of sonofabitch am I, deliberately planning to knock myself off and leave her a widow, without sufficient income, no escort for dinner parties, and defenseless against fuse boxes?

Now that Women's Liberation has come on the scene, dear Washoe, the gulf between us is greater than ever.

Consider, if you will.

We have taken to sharing the household chores. When it is my turn to do the laundry or the dishes, I naturally let them pile up until there is a big enough stack to make it worthwhile. Then I do a whole batch at once.

Will you tell me why this method infuriates her?

For her part, she washes out individual items—by hand! —and never lets so much as a cup or spoon rest in the sink for more than five minutes.

When I point out that my way is more sensible, less time-consuming, less energy-wasteful, she flings back at me: "Two thousand years and more of patriarchy aren't enough for you! You still have to make up the rules so that you can win!"

To Him It May Concern,

I, Washoe, after my initial nineteen words, took upon myself to learn the word "Open" and so make a score.

At first I used it only in connection with a house door. Later I learned that the word could open other closed areas: refrigerator doors, car doors, cupboards and jars.

Do you want me to try to teach the word to your wife?

She Intimates an Opening

EXPanD
contract

flaps of the vulva
parting
the tent widening
held up by
tent-peg clitoris
staking its claim
stronger
driving deep into the
groundswell

into a circle round as an
O

-pen
shut in the clamping enclosure

Enter
making his way
the wandering knight
knocking on the door in
the ivied wall of the convent close
Mother, Sister, open up to me!
O lady lady
in the name of the Father the Son the

wholly taking him in
his plumed helmet
his sword and buckler
twin saddlebags
his foam-spittling horse
his entire retinue
bedded overnight

and in the morning
Inventory

item:
curls from his plumage inside her
item:
hoofbeats thrilling hoofbeats still pounding
as he
lifts
off

WHAT? So Soon? Ah no lord my lad not yet
but he is already buckling himself together
(she has dusted his buckle
   polished his sword
     filled both his bags with fresh-risen bread)
and he is leaving her
spurring his heels
kicking at his steed and HeighHo A-way from
her clitoris-spur clinging
kicking him in
I'm not done for yet   Is this any way to go?
Before I'm half-done with you, boy?
but he's out of earshot
and she stays
inside the close
within the walls

where
she is kept
seeking
Satisfaction
as

people put things in her
babies
bottles
cups
forceps
spoons
broom handles
curtain rods
rulers

they prize her and clam her
she keeps on expanding and contracting

an
open
and
shut
case.

Eumenides

Standing in line at the checkout counter, I overhear them:

One speaks of her husband: "I was playing music on the phonograph, old show tunes, there I was dancing around the room hugging my memories while he got gloomier and gloomier, sinking into his glass, stirring the whiskey and melted ice cubes with his finger. Wouldn't even answer when I asked, 'How about this one, hon? Remember this?' We had danced to it at our wedding. 'Ahh,' he yawned, 'humpity dum dum, they all sound the same.
Who can bother to tell one from the other?'
I grabbed the record off and threw it on the floor so fast that I snapped the arm on the player and broke it.
He jumped up. 'I hate violence,' he said, and grabbed me, slapped me over his knee."

The second woman: "You're lucky. At least he showed he was alive. I still get the silent treatment. It's more than I can stand when he comes home and buries himself in the sports page and the stock market."

Third woman: "They get worse as they age. They need you around every minute. Mine even expects me to take the pins out of his new shirts for him before he puts them on; it's not enough I buy them for him because he doesn't like to shop. I think that's why God has us outlive them. So we can finally enjoy a little peace and freedom for ourselves, even if it's only in picking the TV channel or eating tuna fish casseroles."

They look through me as they wheel their baskets out: unabashed biddies, don't even blush.

Camera Eye

In
an ongoing
series of
candid photographs

men
with their eyes shining
their mouths open
their tongues darting

all
hungrily
leaning toward
the same food:

the picture of
a woman
and how she is
undressed.

In a similar
series of
candid snaps

women
with their eyes shining
mouths open
tongues darting

each one
hungrily
panting toward
the same food:

the picture of
a woman
noting the most microscopic details
of how she is dressed.

Dream Graffiti for
the Ladies' Room

1

She is a table mat
while he
holds the keys to the car.

2

She is a flower
opening   curling   fading
while he is the stem
she is attached to.

3

She is a fork
with prongs that can punch little holes
while his knife
cuts bread and meat
into man-sized pieces.

4

She is an oasis of green tears
leaving him parched
in the bonewhite desert.

5

There are strings on her
but he
is in a bind.

From the Unabridged

Wive, verb transitive
"to bring into close union,
as thoughts with words."

> Why don't you
> ever
> let me know
> what your
> feelings
> really
> are?

Husband, verb intransitive
"to direct or manage with frugality;
to spend, apply, or use with economy;
as to *husband* one's means of strength.
Syn.: eke, conserve, save, store.
Ant.: dissipate, squander, lavish."

> To have
> and to
> withhold.

Swive, verb transitive and intransitive
"Middle English *swiven,*
Anglo-Saxon *swifar* to move, go;
Old Norse *swifa* to ramble.
To copulate."

Wife, noun
"Middle English *wif,*
Old Norse *vif,*
Danish *viv,*

and perh. to Old Norse *vifann* veiled,
veifa to wave,
see VIBRATE."

-*wife,* a combining form
"as in

> applewife
> butterwife
> cocklewife
> fishwife
> goodwife
> henwife
> herbwife
> hostlerwife
> housewife
> kalewife
> midwife
> oldwife
> oysterwife
> piewife
> puddingwife
> roupingwife
> saltwife
> seawife
> washerwife
> witchwife."

Wifething, noun
"Nuptials,
obsolete."

Sparkle Plenty

> *"A good club soda*
> *is like a good woman:*
> *it won't quit on you."*
> —Canada Dry advertisement

Our hostess
stays animated
bubbling

      pouring
      herself the bottle   the good mixer
      herself the tray
      the wipeclean surface

yes Hal's job took us first to Englemont
where Hal Junior was born
and then the company sent him to Ridgewood where
we had Bobby and then
his next job took us to Homestead Heights and
this time the baby was a girl and
do let me pour you out another
no it's no trouble for me at all
and then the miscarriage
and then a preemie
it would have been another girl if it had lived
the doctor said maybe I should stop taking the pill
but I kept getting the same dizziness and blackouts only
a little more
I'm so glad you like it it's really
a simple recipe a straight
D and C no complications
just scraping the walls
and my depression didn't last too long for a

dip you can marinate if you want in a bowl
in the refrigerator and forget about it while you sleep
and then just take it out the next
morning I went to the rest home
that's what it really looks like
flower gardens and cretonne curtains you can't even see the
bars on the windows unless you're looking straight at them
when they took away my cuticle scissors and belts
I was upset but
the baskets I learned to weave
can be used for hanging plants
and it's a good moneysaver
and a worthwhile skill
and he's proud of his best girl Hal said
when he came to take me back to our real home
my clothes hung on me and
my hair was falling out in little clumps
but the wigs nowadays are so natural
and they have their own traveling cases
and the children don't leave all at once
I freeze an extra amount
and then for company
all you have to do is
reheat and then serve
while it is still
bubbling

As we leave the cocktail party, she embraces our effervescent hostess and whispers with her at length. When we get out to the car I ask, What were you doing back there? What was that all about?

"Talking to myself," she answers.

Funerary

Cryogenics interests me, freezing the body for the future. If there were any way to conserve myself after death, for my presence to be restored in the world—and if it were not so expensive—I would try it. For I have been of some weight, some matter; I have supported a family, earning a keep. Lacking the assurance, however, that I could be thawed out for a return, I shall either be cremated or go into the family plot.

She wants to donate her body to the local medical school, has a card for the eye bank, and would like to be guaranteed that she will die with her kidneys intact so that she can pass them on to be recycled.
Why this morbid passion to become a necrophiliac thrift shop?

Let whatever remains of me be used, she cries, let whoever can use me, use me up!

Man-Made Creations

Minerva sprung from Jove's brow

Eve out of Adam's rib

little boys
make up stories
in the dark

in the dark of the cave
the cave of the great goddess
She

Divining

All your life you may have borne the gift
and never known you had it in your nature
because no one ever showed you how to bring it forth:

take a forked branch
of willow or apple
almost any soft wood will do

grasp both ends
firmly but without pressure
like lightly held reins

now stretch your arms out
in front of you at shoulder height
a sleep walker

where are you leading
where are you being led
keep walking

until the branch of its own accord
turns within your hands
and the fork points down to the ground

here a well can be dug
here under this dry surface water flows
here you are in life-giving luck

the gift of divining
has nothing to do with the fates
or witches or maidens or wise old crones

the gift of divining
is human
and can happen to every sex